Science

Reading Support and Homework

Grade 1

Harcourt
SCHOOL PUBLISHERS

Orlando   Austin   New York   San Diego   Toronto   London

Visit *The Learning Site!*
www.harcourtschool.com

Printed in the United States of America

ISBN 0-15-343603-4

9 10 11 12 13 14 15 1421 15 14 13 12 11 10 09

© Harcourt

Contents

Chapter 1 All About Animals

Chapter 2 All About Plants

Our Earth

Natural Resources

Chapter 7 — Measuring Weather

Chapter 8 — Seasons

© Harcourt

Chapter 9 — Objects in the Sky

Chapter 10 — All About Matter

Name_____

Date _____

Welcome to *Science!*

Find these things in your book.

1. What animal is on the cover of your book?
_____
- -
_____

2. How many chapters are in your book?
_____
- -
_____

3. Look on page 4. What word is in a yellow box?
_____
- -
_____

4. How many questions are on page 7?
_____
- -
_____

Name_____

5. Look on page 19. What Inquiry Skill
is shown?

_____

- -

_____

6. Look in the Health Handbook. It is in the
back of your book. On what page do you
find a skeleton?

_____

- -

_____

7. What is the first word in the glossary?

_____

- -

_____

8. Find a picture of something you like.
Tell about it.

_____

- -

_____

_____

- -

_____

Name _____

Date _____

Write to Inform

A. Draw one of your favorite animals.

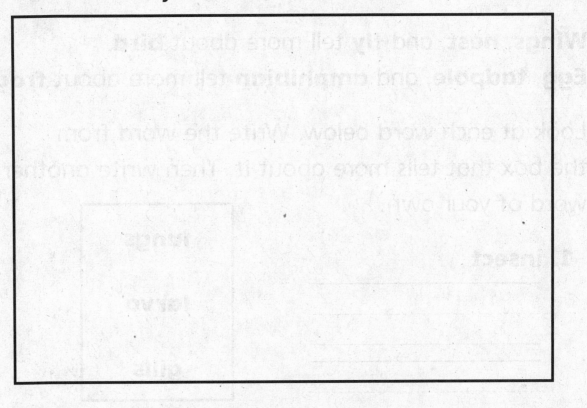

B. Write about the animal you drew. Tell what the animal needs.

_____

- -

_____

_____

- -

_____

© Harcourt

Name_____

Date _____

All About Animals

You can list words that tell more about something.

Wings, **nest**, and **fly** tell more about **bird**.
Egg, **tadpole**, and **amphibian** tell more about **frog**.

Look at each word below. Write the word from
the box that tells more about it. Then write another
word of your own.

1. insect

_____

- -

_____

_____

- -

_____

lungs
larva
gills

2. fish

_____

- - - - - - - - - - - - - - - - - -

_____

_____

- - - - - - - - - - - - - - - - - -

_____

3. mammal

_____

- -

_____

_____

- -

_____

Name_____

Date _____

Lesson 1 - What Are Living and Nonliving Things?

1. Inquiry Skill Practice–Classify

Look at the pictures. Circle each living thing. Mark an X on each nonliving thing.

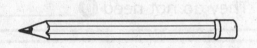

2. Use Vocabulary

Write the word that best completes each sentence.

Living	Nonliving

_____ things do not grow and change.

_____ things grow and change.

© Harcourt

Name_____

3. ⭐(Focus Skill) **Compare and Contrast**

Use this chart with the Reading Review.

Living Things	**Nonliving Things**
They need **A** _____.	They do not need food.
They need water.	They do not need **B** _____.
They need **C** _____.	They do not need **D** _____.
They grow and **E** _____.	They do not **F** _____.

4. **Critical Thinking and Problem Solving**

You grow and change, too. What tools could you use to measure how? Write a plan.

_____

_____

_____

_____

_____

_____

© Harcourt

Lesson 2 - What Do Animals Need?

1. ## Inquiry Skill Practice–Observe

Look at the animals. What need is each meeting? Write about what you observe.

----

2. ## Use Vocabulary

Match the word to the sentence that tells about it.

shelter •   • Fish use these to breathe.

gills •   • This is a place where an animal can stay safe.

lungs •   • Many animals use these to breathe.

© Harcourt

Name_____

3. ⭐Focus Skill | Main Idea and Details

Use this chart with the Reading Review.

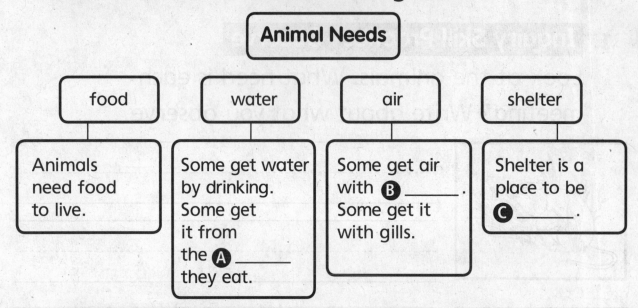

Animal Needs

food	water	air	shelter
Animals need food to live.	Some get water by drinking. Some get it from the **A** _____ they eat.	Some get air with **B** _____ . Some get it with gills.	Shelter is a place to be **C** _____ .

4. Critical Thinking and Problem Solving

Smoke, dust, and other things can make air dirty. Do you think it is important to keep air clean? Write about why you think so.

_____

_____

_____

_____

_____

_____

© Harcourt

Name _____

Date _____

Lesson 3 - How Can We Group Animals?

1. Inquiry Skill Practice–Classify

Label each picture **mammal**
or **reptile**.

   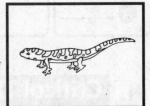

_____   _____   _____   _____

2. Use Vocabulary

Fill in each blank with a word from
the box.

mammal   fish

A _____ is a _____ .

A _____ is a _____ .

© Harcourt

Name_____

3. 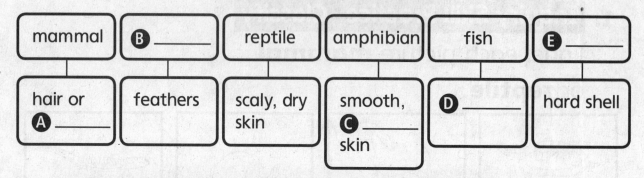 **Main Idea and Details**

Use this chart with the Reading Review.

Animal Body Coverings

mammal	Ⓑ_____	reptile	amphibian	fish	Ⓔ_____
hair or Ⓐ_____	feathers	scaly, dry skin	smooth, Ⓒ_____ skin	Ⓓ_____	hard shell

4. **Critical Thinking and Problem Solving**

Why do you think birds have feathers instead of fur or scales? Write to explain.

_____

_____

_____

_____

_____

© Harcourt

Name_____

Date _____

Lesson 4 - How Do Animals Grow and Change?

1. **Inquiry Skill Practice—Compare**

Think of an animal you know about.
Draw it as a young animal and then
as a grown animal.

young	grown

2. **Use Vocabulary**

Write the word or words that best
complete each sentence.

life cycle	tadpole

A _____ is all the parts of an
animal's life.

A _____ is a young frog.

Name_____

3. (Focus Skill) Sequence

Use this chart with the Reading Review.

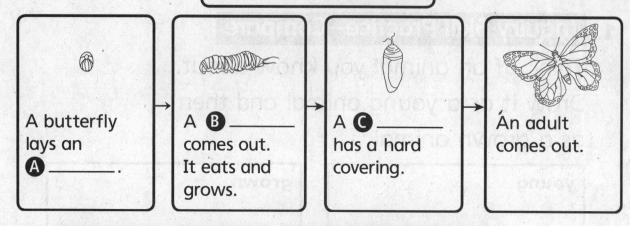

Life Cycle of A Butterfly

A butterfly lays an **A**_____ .

A **B**_____ comes out. It eats and grows.

A **C**_____ has a hard covering.

An adult comes out.

4. Critical Thinking and Problem Solving

Match the young animal with its parent.
Write to tell how you know.

_____

_____

_____

© Harcourt

All About Plants

You can change a word's meaning by adding a beginning or an ending.

The letters **non–** mean **not**.

Non– + edible = **nonedible**.

So **nonedible** means **not** edible.

Add the ending **–less** to the end of each word below.

root _____

fruit _____

seed _____

How does –<u>less</u> change a word?

Draw a <u>leafless</u> tree to show your ideas.

Name_____

Date _____

Lesson 1 - What Do Plants Need?

1. **Inquiry Skill Practice–Predict**

Look at the pictures. Predict what will
happen to each plant after a few days.

I predict this plant will _____.

I predict this plant will _____.

How could you check your prediction?

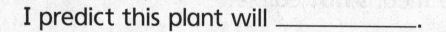
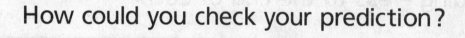

_____

_____

_____.

2. **Use Vocabulary**

Write the word that best completes
each sentence.

sunlight nutrients

Plants get _____ from the soil.

Plants get _____ from the sun.

© Harcourt

Name_____

3. ⭐ (Focus Skill) **Cause and Effect**

Use this chart with the Reading Review.

> **Needs of Plants**

cause

A plant gets light, Ⓐ_____, Ⓑ_____, and nutrients.

↓

effect

The plant grows and stays Ⓒ_____.

4. **Critical Thinking and Problem Solving**

People water house plants. Most plants grow outside. Where does their water come from? Write about two ways plants may get water.

_____

_____

_____

_____

_____

_____

Name_____

Date _____

Lesson 2 - What Are the Parts of a Plant?

1. **Inquiry Skill Practice–Communicate**

Write the name of a plant part to complete this diagram. Communicate to a partner about how each part helps the plant.

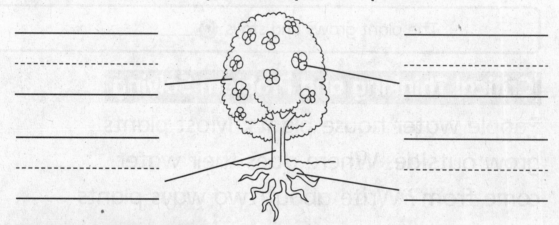

_____   _____

------------------   ------------------

_____   _____

------------------   ------------------

_____   _____

2. **Use Vocabulary**

Complete the chart with words from the list.

roots	stem	fruits

Plant Parts	
name	how it helps a plant
_____	These hold seeds.
_____	This holds up the plant.
_____	These hold the plant in the soil.

© Harcourt

Name_____

3. Main Idea and Details

Use this chart with the Reading Review.

Main Idea and Details

The parts of a plant help it live and grow.

The roots take in **A**_____ and **B**_____ from the soil.	The **C**_____ holds up the plant.	The leaves make **D**____ for the plant.	The flowers make **E**____ . The fruits hold **F**_____ .

4. Critical Thinking and Problem Solving

Why do you think some plants have woody stems? Draw a conclusion. Write to explain.

_____

_____

_____

_____

_____

_____

_____

Name _____

Date _____

Lesson 3 - How Do Plants Grow and Change?

1. **Inquiry Skill Practice–Sequence**

Draw the two missing pictures. Show how the bean plant grows.

first   then   next   last

2. **Use Vocabulary**

Look at this seed. Write a sentence about how the **seed coat** helps the seed.

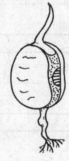

_____

- -

_____

Name_____

3. (Focus Skill) Sequence

Use this chart with the Reading Review.

Life Cycle of A Tree

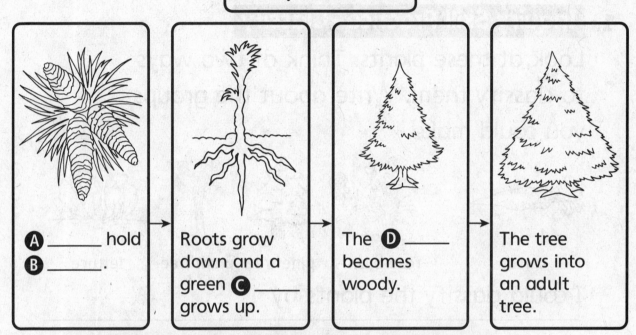

A _____ hold
B _____ .

Roots grow down and a green **C** _____ grows up.

The **D** _____ becomes woody.

The tree grows into an adult tree.

4. Critical Thinking and Problem Solving

You find a seed, but you do not know what kind of plant it came from. How could you find out? Write a plan.

_____

- -

_____

- -

_____

- -

_____

Name _____

Date _____

Lesson 4 - How Can We Group Plants?

1. **Inquiry Skill Practice–Classify**

Look at these plants. Think of two ways to classify them. Write about the groups you could make.

carrot   rose bush   pine tree   plum tree   lettuce

I could classify the plants by
_____
- -
_____.

I could classify the plants by
_____
- -
_____.

2. **Use Vocabulary**

Complete the sentence to tell what the word means.

_____
- -
An **edible** plant _____.

© Harcourt

Name_____

3. (Focus Skill) Compare and Contrast

Use this chart with the Reading Review.

Trees and Shrubs

alike   different

Both have **A**_____ stems.

Most **B**_____ have one big main stem.

C_____ have many smaller stems.

4. Critical Thinking and Problem Solving

Think of something you could make from plants. Write about it. Tell how you would use plants.

_____

- - - - - - - - - - - - - - - - - - -

_____

- - - - - - - - - - - - - - - - - - -

_____

- - - - - - - - - - - - - - - - - - -

_____

- - - - - - - - - - - - - - - - - - -

_____

© Harcourt

Name_____

Date_____

Write to Describe

A. Draw a plant or an animal that lives in each of these places.

forest	_____

desert	_____

ocean	_____

B. Write describing words next to each picture you drew.

© Harcourt

Environments for Living Things

Context clues can help you understand the meaning of a new word.

I saw a bee with **pollen** on it. It picked up the **sticky powder** from a flower.

The words **sticky powder** help you understand what **pollen** is.

Use clues to figure out each underlined word.
Circle the letter that completes the sentence.

1. <u>Oxygen</u> from plants goes into the air.

   <u>Oxygen</u> is _____.

   A a plant's leaves

   B something you can eat

   C something you breathe

2. Some animals use <u>camouflage</u> to hide.

   <u>Camouflage</u> helps animals _____.

   A stay safe

   B find water

   C breathe

© Harcourt

Name _____

Date _____

Lesson 1 - What Is an Environment?

1. ## Inquiry Skill Practice–Communicate

Look at this environment. List things made by people. Communicate with a partner about what you found out.

----

2. ## Use Vocabulary

How can things in an environment be different? Write to explain. Use the word **environment**.

© Harcourt

Name_____

3. Focus Skill Main Idea and Details

Use this chart with the Reading Review.

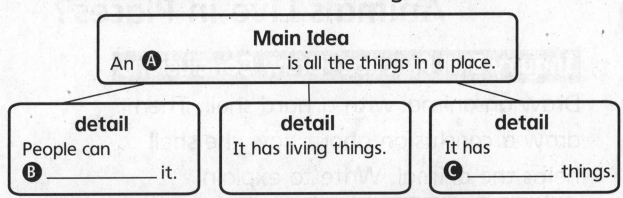

Main Idea

An **A** _____ is all the things in a place.

detail
People can **B** _____ it.

detail
It has living things.

detail
It has **C** _____ things.

4. Critical Thinking and Problem Solving

Near your home is an empty lot. What are ways people could change it? Which one would you like best? Why?

_____
_____
_____
_____
_____
_____

© Harcourt

Name_____

Date _____

Lesson 2 - What Helps Plants and Animals Live in Places?

1. **Inquiry Skill Practice–Draw Conclusions**

Draw an animal with a hard shell. Then draw a conclusion about how the shell helps the animal. Write to explain.

_____

- -

_____

_____

- -

2. **Use Vocabulary**

Fill in each blank with **camouflage** or **adaptation**.

A brown deer may use _____ to hide in brown grass.

A fish may have an _____ to help it move.

© Harcourt

Name_____

3. 🌟 Focus Skill | Compare and Contrast

Use this chart with the Reading Review.

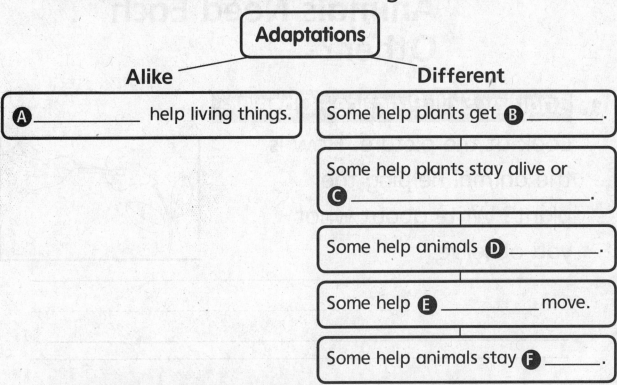

Adaptations

Alike

A _____ help living things.

Different

Some help plants get **B** _____.

Some help plants stay alive or **C** _____.

Some help animals **D** _____.

Some help **E** _____ move.

Some help animals stay **F** _____.

4. Critical Thinking and Problem Solving

Adaptations can help animals live in cold
and hot places. What might help an animal
live in a cold place? Write to explain.

_____

_____

_____

_____

_____

_____

Lesson 3 - How Do Plants and Animals Need Each Other?

1. Inquiry Skill Practice–Observe

Look at the picture. How is the animal helping the plant? Write about what you observe.

_____

_____

_____

_____

2. Use Vocabulary

Match each vocabulary word or words to the sentence that tells about it.

food chain •   • This is a gas.

pollen •   • This comes from flowers.

oxygen •   • This shows how plants
                                 and animals are linked.

Name_____

3. (Focus Skill) **Main Idea and Details**

Use this chart with the Reading Review.

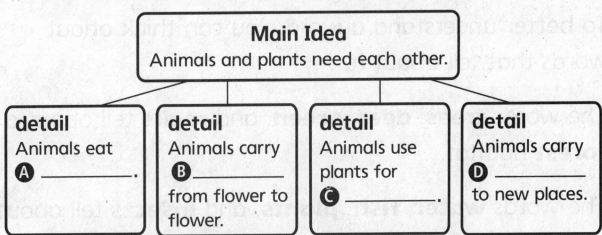

Main Idea
Animals and plants need each other.

detail	detail	detail	detail
Animals eat **A** _____.	Animals carry **B** _____ from flower to flower.	Animals use plants for **C** _____.	Animals carry **D** _____ to new places.

4. **Critical Thinking and Problem Solving**

Draw an animal you know about.
How does the animal use plants? Find
information in books. Write to explain.

animal: _____

_____

- -

_____

- -

Name _____

Date _____

Places to Live

To better understand a word, you can think about words that tell about it.

The words **trees**, **deer**, **green**, and **rocks** tell about a **forest** habitat.

The words **water**, **fish**, **plants**, and **insects** tell about a **pond** habitat.

Add words to each list below. Then draw each habitat. Include all the things from your list in the picture.

ocean habitat	**desert** habitat
fish	dry

© Harcourt

Name_____

Date _____

Lesson 1 - What Lives in a Forest?

1. **Inquiry Skill Practice–Compare**

Compare the two forest plants. Tell how they are alike and different.

alike   different

_____   _____

- - - - - - - - - - -   - - - - - - - - - - -

_____   _____

_____   _____

- - - - - - - - - - -   - - - - - - - - - - -

_____   _____

2. **Use Vocabulary**

Match each word to the sentence that tells about it. _____

| forest habitat |

A - - - - - - - - - _____ is a place where an animal finds food, water, and shelter.

A - - - - - - - - - _____ is land that is covered with trees.

© Harcourt

Name_____

3. Main Idea and Details

Use this chart with the Reading Review.

Forests

Main Idea

A **A** _____ is a place where many trees grow.

detail

Trees get enough rain and
B _____ .
Ferns and forest flowers do not
need much **C** _____ .

detail

Bears need a large part of
the **D** _____ to live in.
Smaller animals may live in
a **E** _____ in the forest.

4. Critical Thinking and Problem Solving

What might happen if people cut down
many of the trees in a forest? Draw a
conclusion. Write to explain.

_____

_____

_____

© Harcourt

Name_____

Date _____

Lesson 2 - What Lives in a Desert?

1. **Inquiry Skill Practice–Draw Conclusions**

Look at this desert plant.
Draw a conclusion about
what helps it live in
the desert.

_____

_____
_____

_____

2. **Use Vocabulary**

Draw a picture of a desert. Then use the
word **desert** to write about your picture.

_____

Name_____

3. (Focus Skill) Main Idea and Details

Use this chart with the Reading Review.

Desert

Main Idea
A desert is land that gets very little **A** _____.

detail
Plants do not need much
B _____.
A cactus holds water in its
C _____.

detail
Doves and hares rest in
D _____ places to stay cool.
A **E** _____ gets water from
the food it eats.

4. Critical Thinking and Problem Solving

Your family is going for a short hike in
the desert. Think about what a desert
is like. What should you bring with you?
Write to explain.

_____

_____

_____

_____

_____

© Harcourt

Name_____

Date _____

Lesson 3 - What Lives in an Ocean?

1. Inquiry Skill Practice–Classify

Classify the ocean animals into two groups.
Circle the animals in one group. Underline the
others. Write about your groups.

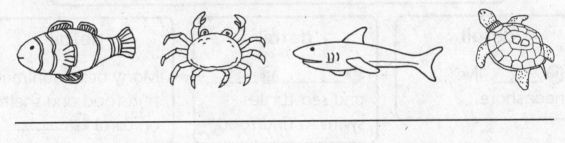

_____

- -

_____

- -

2. Use Vocabulary

Look at this picture. How
do you know it shows
an ocean? Use the word
ocean to explain.

_____

- -

_____

- -

Name _____

3. ★ Focus Skill | Main Idea and Details

Use this chart with the Reading Review.

Oceans

Main Idea
An ocean is a large body of **A** _____.
Ocean animals live where they can find **B** _____.

detail	detail	detail
C _____ live near shore.	**D** _____, **E** _____ and sea turtles swim to find food.	Many ocean animals find food and shelter on coral **F** _____.

4. Critical Thinking and Problem Solving

How is an ocean different from a lake?
Write to explain.

_____
- - - - - - - - - - - - - - - - - - -
_____
- - - - - - - - - - - - - - - - - - -
_____
- - - - - - - - - - - - - - - - - - -
_____
- - - - - - - - - - - - - - - - - - -
_____

© Harcourt

Name _____

Date _____

Write a Story

A. Draw a picture of recycling at your school.

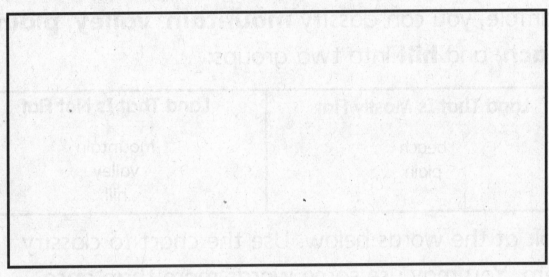

B. Write a story about your picture. Include details about what you observe.

_____
- -
_____
- -
_____
- -
_____
- -
_____
- -
_____

Our Earth

You can classify words by what they mean. For example, you can classify **mountain**, **valley**, **plain**, **beach**, and **hill** into two groups:

Land That Is Mostly Flat	Land That Is Not Flat
beach plain	mountain valley hill

Look at the words below. Use the chart to classify them. You may use some words more than once.

mountain   **beach**   **erosion**
drought   **ocean**   **lake**

Places Where People Go to Swim	Land That May Be Rocky
_____ _____ _____	_____ _____ _____

Things That Can Change Land	
_____ _____	_____ _____

© Harcourt

Name_____

Date _____

Lesson 1 - What Are Some Kinds of Land?

1. Inquiry Skill Practice–Classify

Underline the pictures of beaches. Circle the pictures of plains.

Tell how you know what each picture shows.

_____

- -

_____

2. Use Vocabulary

Answer each question. Use a word from the box.

mountain	valley	plain

_____

What can have a rocky peak? _____

What is the low land between hills? _____

What is a flat land that spreads out? _____

© Harcourt

Name_____

3. Compare and Contrast

Use this chart with the Reading Review.

Earth's Land

alike

All are high lands.

All are low lands.

different

A Ⓐ_____ is the highest kind of land.

A Ⓑ_____ is a high place that is smaller than a mountain.

A Ⓒ_____ is low land between mountains.

A Ⓓ_____ is flat land that spreads out a long way.

A Ⓔ_____ is flat, sandy land along a shore.

4. Critical Thinking and Problem Solving

Where could you look to learn about land in your state? Write a plan.

_____

- -

_____

- -

_____

Name _____

Date _____

Lesson 2 - What Are Some Kinds of Water?

1. Inquiry Skill Practice–Infer

On a car trip, you see a large body of water. It has land all around it. Infer whether it is a stream, river, lake, or ocean. Explain how you know.

_____

_____

_____

_____

_____

2. Use Vocabulary

Label each picture. Tell whether each is a **stream**, **river**, **lake**, or **ocean**.

_____ _____ _____ _____

Name_____

3. Compare and Contrast

Use this chart with the Reading Review.

Earth's Water

alike

All are kinds of water.

different

A **Ⓐ** _____ is a small body of moving water.

A **Ⓑ** _____ is a larger body of moving water.

A **Ⓒ** _____ is a body of still water with land all around it.

An **Ⓓ** _____ is a large body of salty water.

4. Critical Thinking and Problem Solving

Sand may be carried from a mountaintop to the ocean. How do you think this happens? Write to explain.

_____

_____

_____

_____

_____

© Harcourt

Name _____

Date _____

Lesson 3 - How Does Earth Change?

1. **Inquiry Skill Practice–Make a Model**

Think of what happens in a drought.
How could you model a drought with a
tray of soil? Write a plan.

_____

_____

_____

_____

_____

2. **Use Vocabulary**

Fill in the blanks to complete the
paragraph. Use the words from the box.

drought   flood   erosion

Earth can change for many reasons. Moving water

_____

can cause _____. Heavy rains can cause a

_____   _____

_____. Dry weather can cause a _____.

© Harcourt

Name_____

3. (Focus Skill) **Cause and Effect**

Use this chart with the Reading Review.

Earth Changes

| cause | ⟶ | effect |

Heavy rain falls.	⟶	There may be a **A** _____.
No rain falls.	⟶	There may be a **B** _____.
Water moves over land.	⟶	It carries away **C** _____ and **D** _____ to new places.

4. **Critical Thinking and Problem Solving**

Look at this picture. How are the rocks
changing? Why? Write to explain.

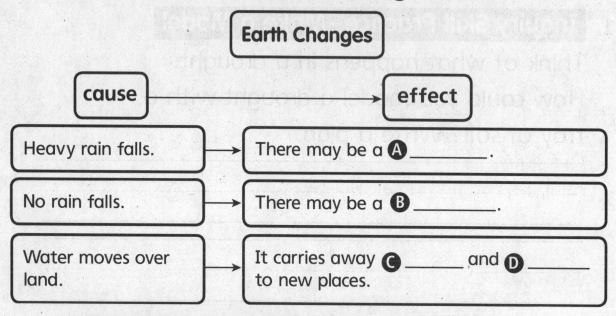

_____

_____
_____

_____

Name _____

Date _____

Natural Resources

<u>Rocks</u>, <u>plants</u>, and <u>animals</u> are all natural resources. <u>Land</u>, <u>water</u>, and <u>air</u> are all hurt by pollution.

Look at the words in this list. Which are natural resources? Which tell about ways to protect natural resources? Fill in the chart.

recycle

humus

soil

reduce

rock

reuse

natural resources

_____

- - - - - - - - - - - - - - - - - - - -

_____

_____

- - - - - - - - - - - - - - - - - - - -

_____

- - - - - - - - - - - - - - - - - - - -

_____

ways to protect natural resources

_____

- - - - - - - - - - - - - - - - - - - -

_____

- - - - - - - - - - - - - - - - - - - -

_____

- - - - - - - - - - - - - - - - - - - -

_____

© Harcourt

Lesson 1 - What Are Natural Resources?

1. **Inquiry Skill Practice–Observe**

Observe your home. What are three things you see that come from natural resources? Make a list.

- _____
  _____
  _____

- _____
  _____
  _____

- _____
  _____

2. **Use Vocabulary**

Use the words **natural resource** to write about this picture.

_____

_____

_____

_____

© Harcourt

Name_____

3. (Focus Skill) Main Idea and Details

Use this chart with the Reading Review.

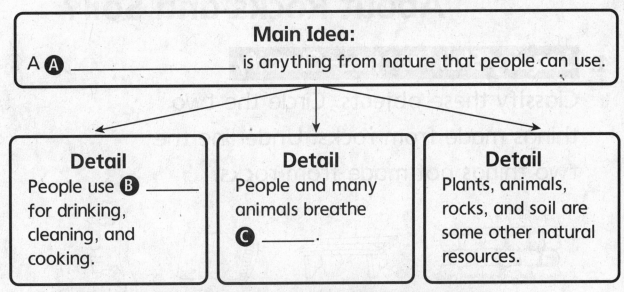

Main Idea:

A (A) _____ is anything from nature that people can use.

Detail
People use (B) _____ for drinking, cleaning, and cooking.

Detail
People and many animals breathe (C) _____.

Detail
Plants, animals, rocks, and soil are some other natural resources.

4. Critical Thinking and Problem Solving

Why are animals a natural resource?
Draw a conclusion. Write to explain.

_____

_____

_____

_____

© Harcourt

Name _____

Date _____

Lesson 2 - What Can We Observe About Rocks and Soil?

1. **Inquiry Skill Practice–Classify**

Classify these objects. Circle the two things made from rocks. Underline the two things not made from rocks.

 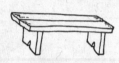 

2. **Use Vocabulary**

Match each word to the sentence that tells about it.

rock •   • This is made of sand, humus, and clay.

soil •   • This is a hard, nonliving thing.

humus •   • This is made of dead plants and animals.

Name_____

3. (Focus Skill) Compare and Contrast

Use this chart with the Reading Review.

Rocks and Soil

alike

All are hard, nonliving things that come from (A)_____.

Soil is made up of sand, (C)_____, and clay.

different

People use rocks to build, to carve into (B)_____ , and to use in food.

Different things, such as roots and rocks, may be in soil.

4. Critical Thinking and Problem Solving

Different plants need different soil mixtures. You are planting bean seeds in pots of soil. How could you find out the best soil mixture for your beans?

_____

_____

_____

_____

Name _____

Date _____

Lesson 3 - How Can We Protect Natural Resources?

1. Inquiry Skill Practice—Draw Conclusions

Mike turns off the water when he brushes his teeth. How does this protect resources?

_____

_____

2. Use Vocabulary

Label each picture with a word from the box.

pollution	recycle

_____   _____

© Harcourt

Name_____

3. (Focus Skill) Cause and Effect

Use this chart with the Reading Review.

Natural Resources

cause ⟶ effect

People make pollution.	⟶	Pollution harms our Ⓐ_____ _____.
People clean up Ⓑ _____.	⟶	People take care of resources.
People Ⓒ _____, reuse, and recycle.	⟶	People make less Ⓓ _____.

4. Critical Thinking and Problem Solving

Think of three new ways you can reduce, reuse, or recycle at home. Write to explain.

_____

_____

_____

_____

_____

© Harcourt

Name _____

Date _____

Write to Explain

Draw your neighborhood as it looks in each season. Write a sentence to explain each picture.

Spring	Summer

_____

_____

_____

Fall	Winter

_____

_____

_____

© Harcourt

Measuring Weather

When you see a new word, look for parts you know.
For example:

What is a **<u>wind</u>sock**?
You know that <u>wind</u> is moving air.
So a **<u>wind</u>sock** might have to do with moving air.

Use word parts to help you figure out the new
words below.

1. A <u>meter</u> is a tool that measures.
A **ther<u>mometer</u>** measures temperature.
Circle words for other measuring tools.

condense anemometer speedometer meeting

2. <u>Vapor</u> is a kind of matter in the air.
Water <u>vapor</u> is water in the air. Circle
other words that tell about matter in
the air.

evaporate weather varnish vaporize

© Harcourt

Name_____

Date _____

Lesson 1 - What Is Weather?

1. **Inquiry Skill Practice–Compare**

Compare the weather in the pictures. Write about what you see.

How is the weather the same?
_____
- -
_____

How is the weather different?
_____
- -
_____

2. **Use Vocabulary**

Write about the weather outside today. Use the word **weather** in your sentence.
_____
- -
_____

© Harcourt

Name_____

3. ⭐ (Focus Skill) Compare and Contrast

Use this chart with the Reading Review.

Weather

alike   **different**

| All weather is what the **A** _____ outside is like. | hot, warm, cool, **B** _____ |

| You can see and **C** _____ all weather. | sunny, **D** _____, rainy, snowy, windy |

4. Critical Thinking and Problem Solving

It is a very rainy, cold day. You have to go outside. What will you wear? Give details.

_____

- -

_____

_____

- -

_____

© Harcourt

Name _____

Date _____

Lesson 2 - How Can We Measure Weather?

1. Inquiry Skill Practice–Measure

Write the temperature shown on each thermometer.

 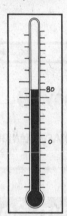 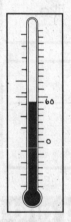

____ ____ degrees Fahrenheit ____ ____ degrees Fahrenheit ____ ____ degrees Fahrenheit

2. Use Vocabulary

Complete each sentence. _____

The **temperature** of air is _____.

A **thermometer** measures _____.

© Harcourt

Name_____

3. (Focus Skill) Main Idea and Details

Use this chart with the Reading Review.

```
┌─────────────────────────────────┐
│        Measuring Weather         │
└─────────────────────────────────┘
```

```
┌──────────────────────────────────────────┐
│                  Main Idea                 │
│    You can measure weather in many ways.   │
└──────────────────────────────────────────┘
```

detail	detail	detail
You can measure **A** _____, which is how hot or cold it is.	You can measure how much **B** _____ has fallen.	You can measure the **C** _____ and **D** _____ of the wind.

4. Critical Thinking and Problem Solving

You want to measure how much rain falls in a week. But if you leave your rain gauge out all week, it may spill over. What can you do? Write a plan.

_____

- -

_____

- -

_____

© Harcourt

Name _____

Date _____

Lesson 3 - What Makes Clouds and Rain?

1. Inquiry Skill Practice–Infer

Infer where the water is in each picture.

I infer that
_____

_____

I infer that
_____

_____

2. Use Vocabulary

Write a word or words from the list to complete each sentence.

> condense
> water vapor

Cool air can cause water vapor
_____
----
to _____.

_____

Water in the air is called _____.

© Harcourt

Name_____

3. (Focus Skill) Cause and Effect

Use this chart with the Reading Review.

The Water Cycle

cause	effect
Sun heats water.	→ Water Ⓐ _____.
Water vapor meets cool air.	→ The cool air makes the water vapor Ⓑ _____.
Water drops get bigger and heavier.	→ Then they fall as Ⓒ _____ or Ⓓ _____.

4. Critical Thinking and Problem Solving

After rain falls, it can flow into rivers and oceans. But what happens to snow after it falls? Write to explain your ideas.

_____

_____

_____

_____

_____

Seasons

Some words can have more than one meaning.

Summer is my favorite **season**.
Mom uses salt to **season** her food.

Each underlined word here has another meaning.
What is it? Use what you know about seasons to
help you.

Do not <u>fall</u> on the ice!
What else can <u>fall</u> mean? Draw and write about your ideas.

_____

- -

_____

The toy had a <u>spring</u> that made it bounce.
What else can <u>spring</u> mean? Draw and write about your ideas.

_____

- -

_____

© Harcourt

Name _____

Date _____

Lesson 1 - What Is Spring?

1. **Inquiry Skill Practice–Hypothesize**

Look at this tree. Hypothesize about how it will change in spring. Tell how you could test your hypothesis.

I hypothesize that _____.

_____

To test it, I could _____.

2. **Use Vocabulary**

Complete the sentence.

_____

Spring is the season when _____

_____

_____.

Name_____

3. (Focus Skill) Main Idea and Details

Use this chart with the Reading Review.

Spring

Main Idea
Spring is one of the four seasons.

detail	detail	detail	detail
The weather gets (A)_____ in spring.	There are more hours of (B)_____ .	Many plants begin to (C)_____ .	Many animals have their (D)_____ .

4. Critical Thinking and Problem Solving

When spring starts, weather may be cool. When spring ends, weather may be warm. How could you observe weather changes in spring? Write a plan.

_____

- -

_____

_____

- -

_____

_____

- -

_____

© Harcourt

Name_____

Date _____

Lesson 2 - What Is Summer?

1. ### Inquiry Skill Practice–Infer

Infer why people wear light clothes in summer. Write to explain.

_____

- -

_____

_____

- -

_____

2. ### Use Vocabulary

Draw a picture that shows **summer**. Write to tell how your picture shows summer.

_____

- -

_____

_____

- -

_____

Name_____

3. Main Idea and Details

Use this chart with the Reading Review.

Summer

Main Idea
Summer is the season after spring.

detail
The weather can be **A**_____.

detail
Some plants grow **B**_____.

detail
Animals have ways to stay **C**_____.

4. Critical Thinking and Problem Solving

One summer day your family goes for a picnic at a lake. It is very hot. What are three ways you might cool off? Explain.

_____

• -
_____

• -
_____

• -
_____

© Harcourt

Name_____

Date _____

Lesson 3 - What Is Fall?

1. Inquiry Skill Practice–Compare

Compare the boy's clothes.

summer   fall

How are the clothes different?

_____

----

2. Use Vocabulary

Complete each sentence with
a word from the box.

| fall | migrate |

_____

Some animals _____ to find food.

Leaves may change color in _____.

© Harcourt

Name_____

3. ⭐(Focus Skill) **Cause and Effect**

Use this chart with the Reading Review.

Fall

cause ——————————————→ effect

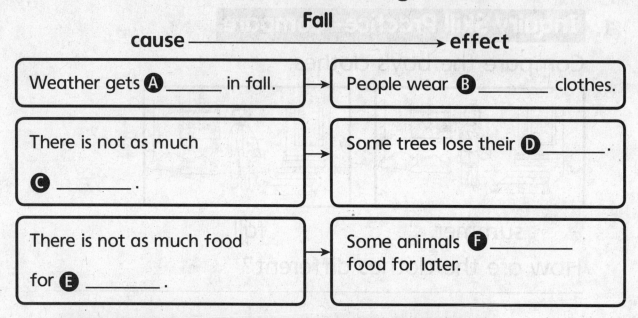

Weather gets **A**_____ in fall. → People wear **B**_____ clothes.

There is not as much

C_____ . → Some trees lose their **D**_____ .

There is not as much food

for **E**_____ . → Some animals **F**_____ food for later.

4. **Critical Thinking and Problem Solving**

These pictures all show an apple tree in fall. They are out of order. Write **first**, **next**, and **last** to tell how the tree changes through fall.

_____ _____ _____

- - - - - - - - - - - - - -   - - - - - - - - - - - - - -   - - - - - - - - - - - - - -

_____ _____ _____

© Harcourt

Name _____

Date _____

Lesson 4 - What Is Winter?

1. **Inquiry Skill Practice–Draw Conclusions**

It can be hard for animals to find food in winter. Draw a conclusion about why. Write to explain.

_____

- -

_____

2. **Use Vocabulary**

Draw a picture that shows **winter**. Write to tell how your picture shows winter.

_____

- -

_____

- -

_____

© Harcourt

Name_____

3. Main Idea and Details

Use this chart with the Reading Review.

Winter

Main Idea
Winter is the season after fall.

detail	**detail**	**detail**	**detail**
The weather may get **A**_____.	In some places, **B**_____ falls.	Plants may rest or **C**_____ .	Some animals grow thick **D**_____ to stay warm.

4. Critical Thinking and Problem Solving

Why do you think it snows in some places in winter and not others? Write to explain.

_____

- -
_____

- -
_____

- -
_____

Name_____

Date _____

Objects in the Sky

Rhyming words have the same ending sounds.

Sk**y** rhymes with wh**y**, cr**y**, tr**y**, fl**y**, sp**y**.
N**ight** rhymes with l**ight**, br**ight**, fr**ight**, s**ight**.

Look at each word. Write words that rhyme. At least one word should be something you can see in the sky.

_____ _____ _____

soon _____ _____ _____

car _____ _____ _____

fun _____ _____ _____

Look at each set of words you wrote. Circle the letters that stand for the same ending sound.

Name _____

Date _____

Lesson 1 - What Can We See in the Sky?

1. Inquiry Skill Practice–Communicate

Draw a picture of the sky at night. Label the objects you drew. Communicate with a friend about your picture.

2. Use Vocabulary

Complete each sentence.

The **sun** is _____.

A **star** is _____.

The **moon** is _____.

© Harcourt

Name _____

3. (Focus Skill) Compare and Contrast

Use this chart with the Reading Review.

Daytime and Nighttime Sky

alike

In the daytime and nighttime sky, you can sometimes see clouds and the moon.

different

In the daytime sky, you may see **A** _____ and the sun.

In the nighttime sky, you may see **B** _____ , planets, and the moon.

In the daytime, the **C** _____ gives off light.

In the nighttime, the stars give off light, but the **D** _____ does not.

4. Critical Thinking and Problem Solving

On a cloudy night, it can be hard to see stars in the sky. Why do you think this is? Write to explain.

_____

- -

_____

© Harcourt

Name _____

Date _____

Lesson 2 - What Causes Day and Night?

1. Inquiry Skill Practice–Make a Model

You could make a model to show how Earth rotates. What materials would you use? How would you do it? Explain.

_____

- -

_____

- -

_____

2. Use Vocabulary

Fill in the blanks to tell how Earth **rotates**.
Use the words in the box.

| day   night   rotates |

When something _____, it spins like a top.
As Earth rotates, the sun lights the sky. Then we

have _____. Earth rotates some more. The

sky gets dark. Then we have _____.

© Harcourt

Name_____

3. (Focus Skill) Cause and Effect

Use this chart with the Reading Review.

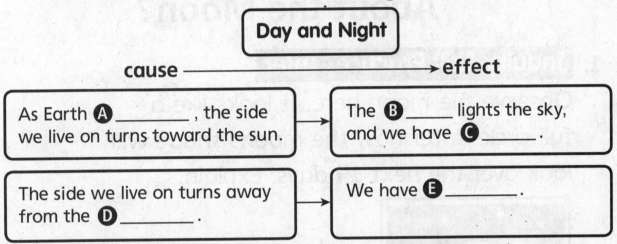

Day and Night

cause ⟶ effect

As Earth **A**_____ , the side we live on turns toward the sun. ⟶ The **B**_____ lights the sky, and we have **C**_____ .

The side we live on turns away from the **D**_____ . ⟶ We have **E**_____ .

4. Critical Thinking and Problem Solving

How could you measure the hours of light in a day? Write a plan.

_____

- -

_____

_____

- -

_____

- -

_____

© Harcourt

Lesson 3 - What Can We Observe About the Moon?

1. Inquiry Skill Practice–Infer

Observe the moon here. It looks like a full circle. Infer how the moon's shape will look over the next 14 days. Explain.

_____

- -

_____

2. Use Vocabulary

Fill in the blanks with details about a **crater**. Use the words in the box.

bowl	moon	surface

You can see them on the _____.

crater

It is a hole in a _____.

It is shaped like a _____.

© Harcourt

Name_____

3. 🌟(Focus Skill) Sequence

Use this chart with the Reading Review.

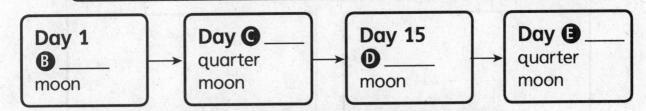

Phases of the Moon

The shape of the **A**_____ seems to change a little each night.

| Day 1
B_____
moon | → | Day **C**_____
quarter
moon | → | Day 15
D_____
moon | → | Day **E**_____
quarter
moon |

4. Critical Thinking and Problem Solving

The moon does not really change shape. It only looks as if it does. Why do you think this is so? Use what you know about how the sun lights the moon to answer the question.

_____

_____

_____

_____

_____

Name_____

Date _____

Write to Compare and Contrast

A. Draw a container of a thin liquid and a container of a thick liquid that you like to drink. Label your pictures.

Thin Liquid: _____	**Thick Liquid:** _____

B. Write about how these liquids are alike.

_____

- -

_____

- -

_____

C. Write about how these liquids are different.

_____

- -

_____

- -

_____

© Harcourt

All About Matter

Think about why the words go together.

hard — soft   up — down

<u>Hard</u> and <u>soft</u> are opposites. Why does <u>up</u> go with <u>down</u>?

How do the first two words go together? Write the word that goes with the third word in the same way.

length	**gas**	**sink**	**liquid**

1. rock — solid   water — _____

2. balance — mass   ruler — _____

3. oil — liquid   air — _____

4. big — small   float — _____

© Harcourt

Name _____

Date _____

Lesson 1 - What Is Matter?

1. **Inquiry Skill Practice—Classify**

Write about ways to classify these
objects.

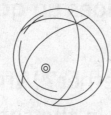

I could classify the objects by

_____

_____

_____

- -

_____

2. **Use Vocabulary**

Draw two different types of **matter** you see
on your desk. Write what you observe.

This matter is	This matter is

© Harcourt

Name_____

3. (Focus Skill) Compare and Contrast

Use this chart with the Reading Review.

Matter

alike   different

Ⓐ _____ is matter.

Matter can be different Ⓑ _____, such as red and yellow.

Matter can be different sizes, such as Ⓒ _____ and Ⓓ _____.

Matter can be different Ⓔ _____, such as circles and squares.

4. Critical Thinking and Problem Solving

Lisa and her father sort clothes before they put them away. Draw to show two things you sort at home. Write what you are doing in each picture.

Lisa and her father sort clothes.

I sort

I sort

© Harcourt

Date _____

Lesson 2 - What Can We Observe About Solids?

1. Inquiry Skill Practice–Compare

Look at the solid objects. Then answer
the questions.

How are the solid objects the same?

_____

_____

How are the objects different?

_____

_____

2. Use Vocabulary

Match the word to the sentence that tells about it.

solid •   • You can measure this with a
                   balance.

mixture •   • This is made up of two or more
                   things.

length •   • This is matter that keeps its shape.

mass •   • You can measure this with a ruler.

Name_____

3. ⭐ Focus Skill **Main Idea and Details**

Use this chart with the Reading Review.

```
┌──────────────┐
│    Solids    │
└──────────────┘
```

```
┌─────────────────────────────────────┐
│              Main Idea               │
│ A solid is matter that keeps its shape. │
└─────────────────────────────────────┘
```

```
┌───────────────────────┐     ┌───────────────────────┐
│ detail                │     │ detail                │
│ You can mix solids.   │     │ You can Ⓐ_____ solids. │
└───────────────────────┘     └───────────────────────┘
```

4. **Critical Thinking and Problem Solving**

Look around you for a mixture. Draw
it. List its parts. Then explain how you
might separate the parts.

This mixture is made up of
_____
- -
_____
- -
_____

I could separate the mixture by
_____
- -
_____
- -
_____

© Harcourt

Lesson 3 - What Can We Observe About Liquids?

1. Inquiry Skill Practice–Measure

Find a container. Will the container hold more than one cup of water? Predict.

_____

_____

_____

How much water does the container hold? Find out. Use a measuring cup.

_____

_____

_____

2. Use Vocabulary

Fill in each blank with a word from the box.

liquid	float	sink

Water is a _____.

A boat will _____ on water.

A heavy rock will _____ in water.

© Harcourt

Name_____

3. (Focus Skill) Main Idea and Details

Use this chart with the Reading Review.

Liquids

Main Idea
A liquid is matter that **A** _____.
It **B** _____ its own shape.

detail
Some matter dissolves in liquids.

detail
Some matter **C** _____, and some floats.

4. Critical Thinking and Problem Solving

Oil is a liquid. Do you think one cup of oil has the same mass as one cup of water? Tell why you think as you do. Then tell how you could find out.

_____
- -
_____
_____
- -
_____
_____
- -
_____

Lesson 4 - What Can We Observe About Gases?

1. **Inquiry Skill Practice–Infer**

Where is the **gas** in this picture? Infer. Then write to tell where the gas is.

_____

- -

_____

- -

How do you know?

_____

- -

_____

- -

2. **Use Vocabulary**

Circle the sentence that tells about **gas**. Underline the sentence that tells about **steam**.

• Air is this.

• This forms when water boils. Tiny drops of water form this.

Name_____

3. (Focus Skill) Cause and Effect

Use this chart with the Reading Review.

Changes in Matter

cause ——————————————→ effect

Water is **A** _____.	→	Water is a liquid.
Water is very cold.	→	Water changes into a **B** _____.
Water is very **C** _____.	→	Water changes into a gas.

4. Critical Thinking and Problem Solving

It is a warm day. There is a pond near your house. Do you think people will be skating on the pond? Why or why not?

_____

_____

_____

_____

_____

_____

Name _____

Date _____

Write Directions

A. Make up a game or a toy that uses magnets. Draw your game or toy in the box.

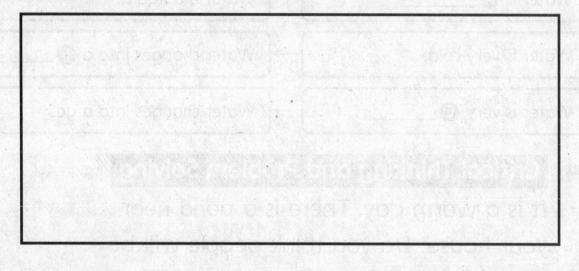

B. Write directions for playing your game or using your toy. Tell what to do first, next, and last.

First _____
_____

Next _____
_____

Last _____

© Harcourt

Heat, Light, and Sound

<u>Heat</u>, <u>light</u>, and <u>sound</u> are all words for **things**. Look how they are used here.

We get <u>heat</u> from the sun.
The lamp gives off a bright <u>light</u>.
The bell made a loud <u>sound</u>.

<u>Heat</u>, <u>light</u>, and <u>sound</u> can also be words for what something **does**. Find out how. Complete these sentences with words from the box.

heat	light	sound

1. Our band will _____ great on Monday.

2. The sun will _____ the water in the pond.

3. Dad will _____ a fire in the fireplace.

© Harcourt

Name_____

Date _____

Lesson 1 - What Is Heat?

1. **Inquiry Skill Practice–Plan an Investigation**

Your schoolyard has a sunny spot. It also has
a shady spot. You want to find out which spot
is warmer. Plan an investigation to find out.

First I would _____

_____

_____

Next I would _____

_____

_____

Last I would _____

_____

_____

2. **Use Vocabulary**

Write to tell about the **heat**
in this picture.

_____

_____

_____

© Harcourt

Name_____

3. (Focus Skill) **Cause and Effect**

Use this chart with the Reading Review.

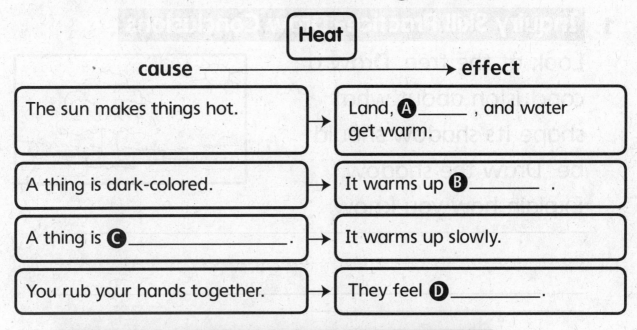

Heat

cause ──────────────→ effect

The sun makes things hot.	→	Land, Ⓐ_____ , and water get warm.
A thing is dark-colored.	→	It warms up Ⓑ_____ .
A thing is Ⓒ_____.	→	It warms up slowly.
You rub your hands together.	→	They feel Ⓓ_____.

4. **Critical Thinking and Problem Solving**

Why is it important to be careful near stoves and ovens? Explain how you know and what you do to stay safe.

_____

- -

_____

- -

_____

Lesson 2 - What Can Light Do?

1. **Inquiry Skill Practice–Draw Conclusions**

   Look at the tree. Draw a
   conclusion about what
   shape its shadow should
   be. Draw the shadow.
   Explain how you know.

   _____

   -

   _____

   -

   _____

2. **Use Vocabulary**

   Complete each sentence to tell about the word.

   Light is
   _____

   -

   _____

   A **shadow** is
   _____

   -

   _____

© Harcourt

Name_____

3. (Focus Skill) **Main Idea and Details**

Use this chart with the Reading Review.

Light

Main Idea
Light is a kind of energy.

detail Light lets us **A**_____ .	**detail** Light can pass through **B**_____ things.	**detail** Light is **C**_____ by things that are not clear.	**detail** When something blocks light, you see a dark **D**_____ .

4. **Critical Thinking and Problem Solving**

You want to read in your room at night.
The light is not bright enough. What
could you do to solve this problem?

_____

- -

_____

- -

_____

© Harcourt

Lesson 3 - What Is Sound?

1. **Inquiry Skill Practice–Hypothesize**

Hypothesize about which bell will make a lower sound. How could you test it?

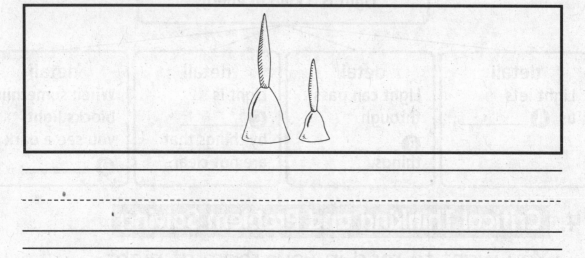

_____

- -

_____

_____

- -

_____

2. **Use Vocabulary**

Complete each sentence with a word from the box.

| pitch   loudness |

A sound's _____ is how loud or soft it is.

A sound's _____ is how high or low it is.

© Harcourt

Name_____

3. ⭐(Focus Skill) **Compare and Contrast**

Use this chart with the Reading Review.

Sound

alike

All sounds are made when something Ⓐ_____.

different

A sound's loudness can be loud or Ⓑ_____.

A sound's pitch can be high or Ⓒ_____.

4. **Critical Thinking and Problem Solving**

You want to make a musical instrument at home. What could you use? How could you do it? Write to explain.

_____

- -

_____

© Harcourt

Motion

Look at each word pair below. The words in
each pair are opposites.

fast — slow   hard — soft
north — south   strong — weak

Now look at the words in this box. Can you find two
pairs of opposites? Write them below.

pull	**repel**	**attract**	**push**

_____   _____

_____ and _____ are opposites.

_____ and _____ are opposites.

Think of another pair of opposites. Write them
on the lines.

_____   _____

_____ and _____ are opposites.

© Harcourt

Name _____

Date _____

Lesson 1 - How Do Things Move?

1. **Inquiry Skill Practice–Classify**

Look at the top, car, train, and pinwheel.
Classify these toys by how they move.

toys that move straight	toys that move in a circle

2. **Use Vocabulary**

Write two sentences about the
picture. Use the word **speed**
in the first sentence. Use the word
motion in the second sentence.

_____

- -

_____

- -

_____

© Harcourt

Use with pages 380–385. (page 1 of 2) **Reading Support and Homework** **RS 95**

Name_____

3. Compare and Contrast

Use this chart with the Reading Review.

Motion

alike	different

All objects in **A**_____ are moving.

The **B**_____ of an object can be fast or slow.

An object may move in a straight path, in a curved path, in a circle, or in a **C**_____.

4. Critical Thinking and Problem Solving

It is not always best to move fast. Think of a time when you may want to move slowly. Write to tell why.

_____

_____

_____

© Harcourt

Name_____

Date _____

Lesson 2 - How Can You Change the Way Things Move?

1. **Inquiry Skill Practice–Plan an Investigation**

Can you move a ball without touching it with your body? Plan an investigation. Write about the steps.

_____

_____

_____

_____

2. **Use Vocabulary**

Complete the sentences to tell about the picture. Use the words **push**, **pull**, and **force**.

Tom and his father use _____ to move objects. Tom uses a _____ _____ to move a box. His father uses a _____ to move the cart.

Name_____

3. (Focus Skill) Cause and Effect

Use this chart with the Reading Review.

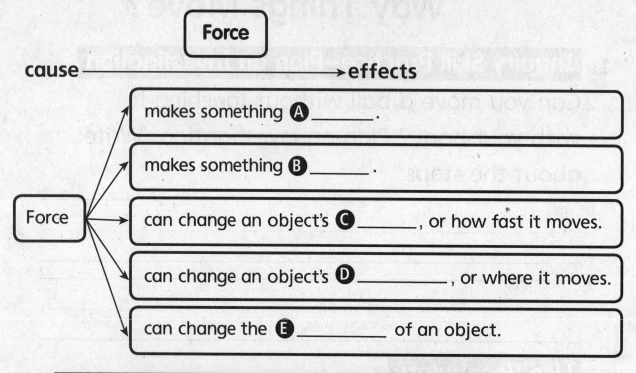

Force

cause ————————————————→ effects

Force

makes something **A** _____.

makes something **B** _____.

can change an object's **C** _____, or how fast it moves.

can change an object's **D** _____, or where it moves.

can change the **E** _____ of an object.

4. Critical Thinking and Problem Solving

A bike can move fast or slow. How can
you change the speed of a bike? Write
to explain.

_____
- -
_____
_____
- -
_____
_____
- -
_____

© Harcourt

Name _____

Date _____

Lesson 3 - How Does Gravity Make Things Move?

1. **Inquiry Skill Practice–Predict**

Look at this picture. Predict what will happen to the ball after the girl throws it.

_____

- -

_____

_____

- -

_____

2. **Use Vocabulary**

Draw a picture that shows gravity pulling an object. Then use the word **gravity** to write a sentence.

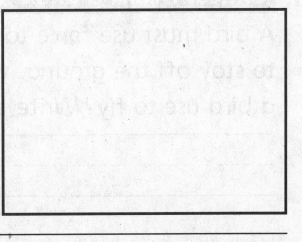

_____

- -

_____

_____

- -

_____

© Harcourt

Name_____

3. ⭐(Focus Skill) **Cause and Effect**

Use this chart with the Reading Review.

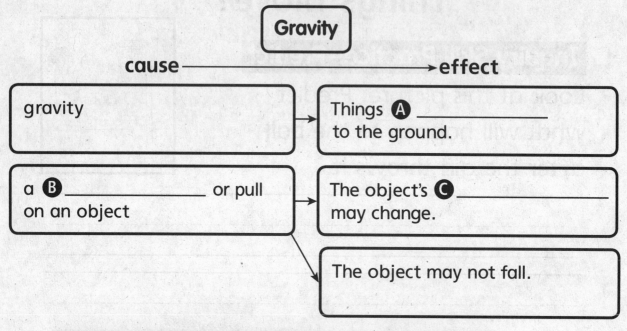

Gravity

cause ————————————→ effect

| gravity | → | Things Ⓐ _____ to the ground. |

| a Ⓑ _____ or pull on an object | → | The object's Ⓒ _____ may change. |

| | → | The object may not fall. |

4. **Critical Thinking and Problem Solving**

A bird must use force to fly. It must work
to stay off the ground. What force does
a bird use to fly? Write to explain.

_____

- -

_____

- -

_____

© Harcourt

Lesson 4 - How Do Magnets Make Things Move?

1. Inquiry Skill Practice–Hypothesize

Will a magnet attract pennies? Hypothesize. Then tell how you could investigate to find out.

_____

- -

_____

- -

_____

2. Use Vocabulary

Match the word to its definition.

an object that attracts iron •   • pole

near the end of a magnet •   • attract

to push away •   • magnetic force

to pull •   • repel

the force a magnet has •   • magnet

Name_____

3. (Focus Skill) ## Main Idea and Details

Use this chart with the Reading Review.

Magnets

Main Idea
A magnet is an object that attracts things made of **A** _____.

detail	detail	detail
A **B** _____ does not pull all metals.	A magnet's pull is called **C** _____.	A magnet's pull is strongest at its **D** _____.

4. ## Critical Thinking and Problem Solving

A drawer has a mix of crayons, markers, paper, and steel paper clips. You want to sort out all of the paper clips. How can a magnet help you? Write to explain.

_____

- -

_____

- -

_____

_____

- -

_____

© Harcourt

VOCABULARY GAMES
and CARDS

Contents

Note to Teachers: The vocabulary cards are listed in alphabetical order for each chapter. These cards are also provided in a different format in *Teaching Resources*. The two formats vary in order to assist with your photocopying needs.

© Harcourt

Vocabulary Games

You can use the word cards on pages RS107–RS160 to play these games.

Get Off My Back!

You will need word cards, tape, paper, and pencil

Grouping whole class, large group, or small group

1. Tape three word cards to another player's back. Do not let that player see the words. Have that player tape three cards to your back. Everyone playing the game should have three word cards taped to his or her back.

2. Ask other players to give hints about each word on your back. Guess each of the three words.

3. If you guess a word correctly, move the word from your back to the front.

4. The player that is the first to move all three words to the front is the winner.

Word Square

You will need word cards, paper, pencil, and crayons

Grouping individuals

1. Fold a sheet of paper in half. Fold it in half again to make four boxes.

2. Choose one word card. In the first box, write the word.

3. In the second box, draw a picture to show what the word means.

4. In the third box, write a sentence to tell what the word means.

5. In the fourth box, draw a picture to show what the word does NOT mean.

Quick Draw

You will need word cards, paper, pencil, and crayons

Grouping whole class, large group, or small group

1. Shuffle word cards. Place them in a stack face down. Draw one card from the stack. Do not show the word to the group.

2. Draw a picture of the word. Ask group members to guess the word.

3. If the word is still not known, give one clue about the meaning of the word. Ask group members to guess the word.

4. The person who guesses the word first gets to keep the word card. The person with the most word cards at the end of the game is the winner.

© Harcourt

senses

inquiry skills

amphibian

science tools

senses

see

smell

taste

hear

touch

The five **senses** are sight, hearing, smell, taste, and touch.

inquiry skills

People use **inquiry skills** to find out information.

amphibian

A frog is an **amphibian**.

science tools

People use **science tools** to help find information they need. A thermometer is a **science tool**.

gills

bird

insect

fish

gills

gills

The **gills** of a fish take air from the water.

bird

A **bird** is the only kind of animal that has feathers.

insect

An **insect** is a kind of animal that has three body parts and six legs.

fish

A **fish** is a kind of animal that is covered in scales, uses gills to breathe, and lives in water.

living

larva

lungs

life cycle

living

People are **living** things.

lungs

Some animals use **lungs** to breathe air.

larva

The **larva** of a butterfly is a caterpillar.

life cycle

All the parts of an animal's or plant's life are its **life cycle.**

pupa

mammal

reptile

nonliving

pupa

A caterpillar becomes a **pupa** before it changes into a butterfly.

mammal

A dog is a **mammal**.

reptile

A snake is a **reptile**.

nonliving

Rocks are **nonliving** things.

edible

shelter

flowers

tadpole

edible

Something **edible** is safe to eat.

shelter

A chipmunk finds **shelter** in a hollow tree.

flowers

flowers

Flowers make fruits.

tadpole

A young frog is a **tadpole**.

RS 116

© Harcourt

nonedible

nutrients

fruits

leaves

nonedible

Something that is not safe to eat is **nonedible**.

fruits

Fruits hold seeds.

nutrients

Plants need **nutrients** from the soil.

leaves

leaves

A plant makes food in its **leaves**.

seeds

roots

stem

seed coat

seeds

New plants grow from **seeds**.

stem

A **stem** holds up a plant.

roots

Plants take in water through their **roots**.

seed coat

The **seed coat** protects a seed.

camouflage

sunlight

environment

adaptation

camouflage

Camouflage is an animal's color or pattern that helps it hide.

sunlight

Light that comes from the sun is **sunlight**.

environment

The **environment** is all the living and nonliving things in a place.

adaptation

An **adaptation** is a body part or behavior that helps a living thing.

pollen

food chain

desert

oxygen

pollen

Pollen is a powder that flowers need to make seeds.

food chain

A **food chain** shows how animals and plants are linked by what they eat.

desert

A **desert** is a place that gets very little rain.

oxygen

Oxygen is a kind of gas that plants give off and animals need to breathe.

ocean

forest

beach

habitat

ocean

An **ocean** is a large body of salt water.

forest

A **forest** is a place with many trees..

beach

A **beach** is the land along the shore of an ocean or a lake.

habitat

An animal finds food, water, and shelter in its **habitat**.

flood

drought

hill

erosion

flood

Too much rain can cause a **flood**.

drought

A **drought** is a long time without rain.

hill

A **hill** is a high place that is smaller than a mountain.

erosion

Erosion can move rocks and soil to new places.

plain

lake

river

mountain

plain

Land that is flat and wide is a **plain**.

lake

A **lake** is a body of water with land all around it.

river

A **river** is a large body of moving water.

mountain

A **mountain** is the highest kind of land.

humus

stream

natural resource

valley

humus

Humus is pieces of dead plants and animals in soil.

stream

A **stream** is a small body of moving water that flows downhill.

natural resource

Water, land, and air are **natural resources.**

valley

A **valley** is found between mountains.

reduce

pollution

reuse

recycle

reduce

Write on both sides of a paper to **reduce** how much you use.

pollution

Pollution is waste that harms the air, water, or land. Fish in a river can be harmed by **pollution**.

reuse

Reuse a jug to make a bird feeder.

recycle

You can **recycle** cans.

condense

rock

evaporate

soil

condense

Water vapor will **condense** into liquid water.

rock

Some walls are made of **rock**.

evaporate

Liquid water will **evaporate** into water vapor.

soil

Soil is made of sand, humus, and clay.

water cycle

temperature

water vapor

thermometer

water cycle

The **water cycle** is how water moves from Earth to the air and back again.

temperature

You can measure **temperature** with a thermometer.

water vapor

Water vapor is water in the air that you can not see.

thermometer

Use a **thermometer** to measure temperature.

migrate

weather

season

fall

migrate

Animals **migrate** to new places to find food.

weather

Weather can be sunny, cloudy, rainy, or windy.

season

The four **seasons** are summer, fall, winter, and spring.

fall

In **fall**, the temperature of the air begins to get cooler.

winter

spring

crater

summer

winter

Winter is the coldest season.

spring

April and May are **spring** months.

crater

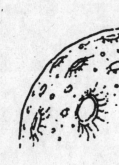

A moon **crater** forms when the moon is hit by a rock.

summer

Summer is the warmest season.

moon

star

rotate

sun

star

A **star** is an object in the sky that gives off its own light.

moon

The **moon** is the brightest object in the night sky.

sun

The **sun** is the closest star to Earth.

rotate

It takes 24 hours for Earth to **rotate** once.

gas

dissolve

length

float

© Harcourt

gas

A **gas** is matter that does not have its own shape. Air is a **gas.**

dissolve

Sugar **dissolves** in water.

length

Length is the measure of how long a solid is.

float

A boat **floats** on water.

matter

liquid

mixture

mass

matter

Matter is everything around you.
Matter can be a solid, liquid, or gas.

liquid

A **liquid** is matter that takes the shape of its container. Juice is a **liquid**.

mixture

A bowl of cereal and fruit is a **mixture**.

mass

Mass is the amount of matter in an object. The elephant has more **mass** than the bird.

steam

sink

heat

solid

steam

When water boils, it becomes a gas called **steam**.

sink

A weight will **sink** to the bottom of a tank.

heat

Heat is a kind of energy that makes things hotter.

solid

A **solid** is a kind of matter that keeps its shape. A penny is a **solid**.

pitch

light

shadow

loudness

pitch

The **pitch** of a sound is how high or low a sound is. The boat has a lower **pitch** than the bird.

light

Light is a kind of energy that lets us see.

shadow

A **shadow** is a dark place made when an object blocks light.

loudness

Loudness is how loud or soft a sound is.

attract

sound

force

vibrate

attract

A magnet will **attract** things made of iron.

sound

Sound is a kind of energy that you hear.

force

A **force** makes an object move or stop moving.

vibrate

The strings will **vibrate** when the guitar is plucked.

magnetic force

gravity

motion

magnet

magnetic force

A **magnetic force** attracts the paper clips to the magnet.

gravity

Gravity pulls things down to the ground.

motion

Motion happens when something moves. The **motion** of a merry-go-round is in a circle.

magnet

A **magnet** will attract things made of iron.

pole

push

pull

repel

push

You **push** a football when you throw it.

pole

A magnet is strongest at its **poles.**

repel

Like poles of two magnets **repel.**

pull

You **pull** a wagon to move it.

speed

speed

Speed is the measure of how fast something moves.